MICHAEL BURRELL

HESS

AMBER LANE PRESS

All rights whatsoever in this play are strictly reserved and application for performance, etc., should be made before rehearsal to:
June Epstein Associates,
32 Shaftesbury Avenue,
London W1V 7DD.

No performance may be given unless a licence has been obtained.

First published in 1980 by
Amber Lane Productions Ltd.,
Amber Lane Farmhouse,
The Slack,
Ashover, Derbyshire S45 0EB

Printed in Great Britain by
Cotswold Press Ltd., Oxford.

Front cover photograph: Michael Burrell as Hess (*courtesy of the BBC, London*)

ISBN 0 906399 18 1

HESS was first performed at the Young Vic Theatre, London, in July and August, 1978, directed by Philip Grout and with the author, Michael Burrell, as Rudolph Hess.

The same production received its American premiere at the Shelter West Theatre, New York, in June, 1979 and subsequently ran at the Eighteenth Street Playhouse and the Entermedia Marquee Theatre from October-December the same year.

Tony Kinnie

For any piece of writing there is seldom a single motive, unless the intention is propaganda. Certainly in writing HESS I was conscious of several motives, not the least of which was to write a play which would stimulate, entertain, move and, perhaps best of all, provoke ideas and questions which would remain with the audience for some time after they had left the theatre. I say a 'play' since, despite the fact that there is only one character, that is how I think of it: it is, after all, set in precisely the location where the performance takes place and the audience is not at a peep-show, or looking through a fourth wall, nor for as long as the subject is alive, is it asked to step back in time. The presence and responses of the audience are acknowledged and at least one member participates by helping Hess with his jacket at the beginning of the second half; so they are integral to the performance and in that sense as much part of the play as Rudolf Hess is.

When I first started to try and construct the piece I was intending to have more than just the one character on stage, but I ran up against two problems. The first was to shape a play which was not an imitation of an existing work, and there have been a lot of plays about prisoners: the interrogation or the court room can be exciting, but they are both rather hackneyed formulas. Setting it in Spandau, where the real Hess is actually held, brought me dangerously near to '*A Nazi for all Seasons*'. Then I had what I thought was a marvellous idea: one actor to play all four guards who rotate their duties at Spandau—

the Russian, the British, the French, the American. With luck it would be a splendid part for the actor concerned and would add an edge to the four different relationships —and then it dawned on me that I should end up with '*The Love* (or more likely, *The Hate*) *of Four Sergeants*'.

The other problem was the character of Hess himself. What attracted me to him as a subject was his oddity, the grim clownishness of his history. A man who was educated, intelligent, by all accounts very civilized in his personal dealings with people including those who worked for him, who not merely obtained power as a leading member of one of the most brutish regimes in history, but who applied that power, albeit at arm's length, with fanatical ruthlessness. A man who protected his own Jewish friends while educating Hitler in the perverse niceties of geo-political imperatives; the ravings of Rosenberg and Streicher, the practical evil of Heydrich, Himmler and their cohorts are, and were at the time, obviously obscene; Hess's contribution was subtler, and in some ways more dangerous and more culpable: he gave anti-Semitism a quasi-respectable cover, and many who should have known better acquiesced or accepted it as a result. Yet ironically he was acquitted of 'Crimes against Humanity' at Nuremberg. The man whose unswerving devotion to Hitler has withstood almost forty years of imprisonment and whose disgust at those who disobeyed the Führer is on record and who, at the same time, committed as flagrant an act of disobedience as was possible by secretly flying to Scotland in 1941. (I discount Hugh Thomas's theory that it was a double who arrived in Hess's place. A conspiracy shared by *both* protagonists in a war and from which neither benefitted or even tried to benefit is a fairly absurd premise, never mind the gaping holes elsewhere in Thomas's argument, such as the evidence of Frau Hess, Albert Speer and the late Ivone Kirkpatrick that the man in Spandau is the one they were all closely familiar with before the war, and the sheer unlikelihood of anyone enduring thirty-nine years in jail without once complaining that his captors had got hold of the wrong fellow.)

These and other ironies in his character and life interested me in him as a dramatic figure. Since, however, I in no way share his political views and would consequently not be shaping some message of which he would approve, and since as a prisoner he is not allowed to read or deny what is written about him, I felt honour-bound to be as true as I could be to the real man in the words I did put into his mouth and in the behaviour I ascribed to him. And this was the problem. Hess is generally a very taciturn man, walking away from conversations he dislikes and often simply not bothering to reply to questions. I needed, therefore, to invent a situation where it was likely that he would want to talk. Confronted by a group of strangers silently looking at you is a situation where I think most individuals would feel inclined to say something, especially as time wore on. And for Hess of course it would bring back memories of other platforms on which he had stood in palmier days. So, I thought, let's suppose that Hess has been spirited by sympathisers from a Military Hospital to the theatre, and there he comes face-to-face with the first crowd of people he has seen since the Tribunal at Nuremberg. The real man has, after all, been out of Spandau and into a Military Hospital on many occasions. And this premise would give an immediacy to the proceedings and a convincing motive for Hess's willingness to talk: it would be his one opportunity. In an age when a confessed spy can be appointed Surveyor of the Queen's pictures, and when a convicted spy can be successfully spirited by helicopter from the top security wing of Wormwood Scrubs, such a happening is more than plausible.

So it was that both problems were resolved by presenting the man alone, with the added advantage that his situation on stage mirrored his situation in prison.

If the argument of the play was to have any value it was obviously important that as many details as possible should be accurate, not easy when I found that of four major histories of the period which I re-read, two erred in such a salient matter as whether or not Hess was found guilty of 'Crimes against Humanity'. For general background I found Shirer's *Rise and Fall of the Third Reich* and Speer's *Inside the Third Reich* valuable and mutually illuminating. Fascinating too was Shirer's *Berlin Diary*. And no doubt countless other books I have read, by Bullock and Trevor-Roper, by Niebuhr, by Isherwood and Tony Parker for example, have shaded my views and left their own imprint. I waded through chunks of *Mein Kampf* (recommended only for hyperinsomniacs), paid helpful visits to the Imperial War Museum and Duxford Aerodrome; consulted Wood and Dempster's *The Narrow Margin* and, in person, John Messerschmitt (who, I hasten to add, spent *his* war in B47s) on the technical details of the Me 110 and even built a model of the thing to make sure I had the 'feel' of it right. I was already familiar with much news-reel of the rallies and trials at Nuremberg, and of the appalling discoveries when the concentration camps were liberated. And Bad Godesberg I knew from my own days as a National Serviceman in the late fifties, which is when the seeds of the play HESS were probably first planted. Among my many German friends was a family who were very kind to me but who turned out, after I had known them for some time, still to be passionate Nazis. Part of my desire to write the piece was to try and resolve how it is that an individual can be personally so generous and principled, and politically so unprincipled and vicious.

On the Nuremberg Trial and its background Andrus's *The Infamous of Nuremberg* was sometimes useful, as was the more scholarly *Reaching Judgment at Nuremberg* by Bradley F. Smith. And the criticisms of the trial which Hess expresses in the play are in some instances close to those recorded in his personal notes by the unimpeachable deputy British Judge at Nuremberg, Lord Birkett.

On Spandau I read Fishman's *Seven Men of Spandau* and two invaluable source-books: Eugene Bird's *The Loneliest Man in the World* and Albert Speer's *Spandau: The Secret Diaries*.

To all these authors I am grateful, and for the story of the British kidnap plot, which is not to be found in any book, I am particularly obliged to a friend of mine, a well-known actor and television presenter who was one of the officers involved and is named as such in the play, though without his giveaway Christian name of McDonald.

But while historical accuracy is important for the play's authority, HESS is not intended as a documentary nor simply as a character study of a failed totalitarian. Both are ingredients, but the mixture of arrogance, self-justification, honesty, twisted logic, blindness and perception with which Hess is characterized in the play allowed me to touch at least on wider issues. And for me the central questions, the abiding questions—and I hope audiences and readers alike will find it the case too—are those concerned with the nature of justice, judgement, suffering, guilt; with whether it is a mistake to think that punishment should reflect only the crime for which it is imposed and take no account of the dignity and values of those who impose it; and with whether, in his assessment of the political ethic, the maligned Machiavelli may not have been absolutely right, absolutely all of the time. I hope not, but it's worth asking.

Finally, my thanks to Philip Grout who directed the play with his customary intelligence and sensitivity, to Tony Kinnie for his critical and practical encouragement throughout this and other enterprises, and to Amber Lane Press who not only have 'the courage of their convictions' but make an impressively snappy decision too.

Michael Burrell
Cambridge, 1980

Select Bibliography

Andrus, Burton C. *The Infamous of Nuremberg*
(1969, Frewin)

Bird, Eugene K. *The Loneliest Man in the World*
(1974, Secker & Warburg)

Fishman, Jack *The Seven Men of Spandau*
(1954, W. H. Allen)

Shirer, William *Berlin Diary* (1941, Hamish Hamilton)

Shirer, William *The Rise and Fall of the Third Reich*
(1960, Secker & Warburg)

Smith, Bradley F. *Reaching Judgment at Nuremberg*
(1977, Basic Books, USA)

Speer, Albert *Spandau: The Secret Diaries*
(1976, Wm. Collins)

Thomas, W. Hugh *The Murder of Rudolf Hess*
(1979, Hodder & Stoughton)

Wood, D. & Dempster, D. D. *The Narrow Margin*
(1961, Arrow Books)

ACT ONE

HESS *comes in wearing pyjamas, dressing gown, raincoat and slippers. In his hand he has a plastic bag holding a plastic milk container. He reacts against the bright lights and the sight of so many people.*

My stomach hurts. Is this a dream or a nightmare? They poison my food. They always poison my food.

[*Slowly he looks round.*]

So, this is your ... Well, as this is my only chance—hello, faces. I don't see so many faces.

[*He moves to the desk upstage centre, puts the plastic bag on it and with difficulty removes his raincoat, putting it also on the desk. He grasps the back of the nearest chair.*]

You of course know who I am. And who I have been. For many years. I'm an Egyptian! I am probably the most famous Egyptian in the world. Maybe President Sadat, Farouk, Cleopatra are coming in the same group. You didn't know I was an Egyptian, did you? You know my name. Hess! Rudolf ... I was born in Alexandria. 26th April, 1894. That means I was almost born under the sign of Aries. Like Adolf Hitler and your beloved Queen Elizabeth II. Or is she Elizabeth I?

So, I was *nearly* an Arian, though of course in another way I'm *really* an Aryan. My father was a merchant. German. I went to school in Alexandria. Had a private tutor at home as well. And I remember, let me see ... I remember my brother being born; and I remember my

15

parents giving me a present. A little toy carriage, drawn by horses. A gun carriage.

When I came back to Germany—all my life I go from Germany and I come back—maybe twice only, but it's all my life. I came back to the Evangelisches Pädagogium at Bad Godesberg. Then I went to Switzerland ... oh, so it's three times, anyway. No, it's more, much more! In Switzerland I was at an École Supérieure to study business. But I don't like business. So I come back and go to Hamburg. To work in business.

Then, you see, war broke out, in your country and in my country. 1914. As a young upstanding German, I volunteered for the First Bavarian Regiment. Wounded three times! [*sheepishly*] Wounded twice. Joined the Air Corps, commissioned as a Leutnant in the Air Corps. I took to flying straight away. It's a natural thing with me, always good at it, always liked it. I have a ... [*He taps his forehead.*] ... technical mind, you see.

Of course, I didn't win the Blue Max—*pour le mérite*—like Göring—Göring was a flyer with me in the same Group—but I got good campaign medals. When my General presented them ... [*mystified*] ... it was muddy ... [*recalling why*] ... we were behind the lines; as he pinned them on, he said, "Well done Hess." "Well done Hess," he said.

> [*This trails off, as Hess goes into a reverie, quite immobile. Then, quite suddenly and brightly*:]

Now I feed the birds. It's as near as I can get. Two times a day I go out and feed them crumbs. [*He demonstrates.*] They come and wait specially for me. Sparrows and all sorts. I try to have something for each one of them. Not the crows. I don't like the crows, they are selfish. They're afraid of the seagulls, though, you know that? The seagulls are smaller, but when they come the crows all fly away. Nations aren't like that. When you invade a

country most of the people don't fly away. Even when it's
hopeless, they have no proper weapons, they still try
to fight.

> [*He bangs a withered fist against the palm of his other
> hand.*]

The crows push everyone around, then, when the going's
not so good, whoosh! ... off they go! No man would do
that. No real man would do that. The birds are the only
freedom of the air I have now.

> [*He looks around as if at the birds, and then begins to
> take in his real surroundings: the lights, the people, the
> furniture. Something about the desk—a half-open
> drawer—catches his attention. He investigates. Then
> he slams the drawer shut.*]

My experiences of the war were like any soldier's,
airman's. Comradeship, privation, discipline, ideals,
love of our homeland. When the war ended we had
nothing—which is more than I had when the next war
ended. Maybe it was necessary. You see, we never
wanted war, we never wished for war. Only Victory.

> [*He is troubled briefly by stomach cramps.*]

[*pathetically*] Why am I here? Oh, I know. Because you
want to hear ... Hess. [*aggressively*] What do you know
about Hess? Huh?—Apart from what I already told you:
born in Alexandria, I worked in Hamburg, I served in the
First World War. [*suddenly reflective*] My family lived in
Bad Godesberg, where the ancient Teutonic Gods, Thor
and Odin, once played. It's a pretty little town, bordering
the Rhein, with small hills and a ferry across to Königs-
winter, I expect that's still the same. Of course they'll be
more people there now: sixty thousand, perhaps seventy
thousand, I don't know. It's been so long I probably
wouldn't recognize it. From the papers I know it's very
'diplomatic'—oh yes, I read four newspapers almost
every day, otherwise I should be quite lost; always two

German papers, then French or British or American ones, depending whose month it is to run the prison. I don't read the Russian papers. They make up the news just like they make up their stupid alphabet. So I know a little about Godesberg, where they give concerts for visiting dignitaries in these days. It's so near to Bonn, hm?

Yes, where should I be without newspapers and music? I like good music: Schubert, Haydn, the Beatles. Why you laugh? You think the Beatles is not good music? But Haydn is the best, especially his String Quartet in C.

> [*He pauses, listening to the music in his head. Then he breaks in on it, bitterly*:]

Oh yes, and you know something else about me. I was Hitler's Deputy, and should by rights be ruling the German Reich, now! I repeat …

> [*He cannot bring himself to say it again.*]

Instead I'm in prison. Since 1941. I have been in prison longer than some of you have been born. Sit back and remember.

> [*He sits.*]

Remember your first day at school? When the desks seemed so big? Strange buildings with a strange smell— Spandau smells a little like that too, with green paint up to here, and then cream. Remember making your first friends in the schoolyard, or, er 'playground'? And tests and teachers? I was here then. Remember sitting your examinations, going to your next school, starting again? I was here. And when you went back to your old school, how small the desks seemed—? Remember going through your Hochschule, graduating, leaving; going maybe to your professional, vocational training, University—I went to University after the First War, the University of Munich. Remember getting your first job, maybe moving from one town to another? Maybe to another country. Remember meeting a girl? Falling in love with her, getting married, having children—or perhaps you did it the other way round; seems to be the fashion nowadays. Remember seeing them, your children, start school? And then remember that every minute of every hour of every day of every one of those memories, I have been a prisoner. Alone in a cell. Because I fought for what I believed in. Because I had the courage of my convictions.

They've given the Nobel Prize to Sadat and Begin—for what? They gave it to Willi Brandt: if I had succeeded in my mission in 1941 I would have done more for world peace than Willi Brandt ever did. He and I were both fugitives in the War. He is an honoured man. I am in Spandau.

We both have sons—I think he has a son ... I don't remember. Mine was three when I left. He's a middle-aged boy now. I didn't see him for twenty-eight years. I couldn't face the shame. I didn't want Wolf to see his father in humiliation. A boy should have better thoughts of his father than that. Then I realized I should die in Spandau, however long I lived. They'll never let me out. So I made a decision! I saw my family. It is allowed for half an hour a month. Six hours in a year. I am a married man who is allowed to share one seven hundred and twentieth of his life with his family. And I'm grateful. I have no choice but to be grateful. Of course I'm not allowed to touch him. It is impermissible for me to caress a hair on his head since he was a toddler.

That very first time they both came, as they entered the room I stood up: "Ilse," I cried, "I kiss your hand." [*He mimes blowing a kiss.*] Wolferl grabbed her arm. "Don't touch him, Mutti," he said. Wolf was right. He knew the rules. Am I that evil? After so long, when I'm so old? Christ touched the lepers but you don't allow anyone to touch me!

19

[*He moves to the stacked chairs up left and sits on the spare one. For some time he remains still, hunched and silent. Then he remembers the audience and stares across at them.*]

I like sitting quiet sometimes. When you're in prison for nearly forty years, you better like sitting quiet. Then I can think. Think about the past. I can only think about the past, I have no present. And I've not had a future for many years now—because they're afraid to let me out, you know that? I am the most expensive prisoner in the world! The governments of four nations provide—oh— 140 men to guard me, and then there are cooks and plumbers *und so weiter*. The most fortified prison in the world *to keep me*! Oh, ja! Dönitz is dead. Räder, Funk, von Papen, they're all dead. Quite a few of the guards are dead, too; they died of the wait—and of the overweight, they have nothing to do but eat; they've all gone. Von Schirach and Speer, they went out in ... they went out in ... they went out. They were free. Since then, I am in solitary confinement not just in my cell. I have a whole prison! A castle among prisons! Don't misunderstand me. I've learned to bear it. It's something you have to do, when you believe like I believe. And I don't mind. Because it's evidence of their fear. Excuse me.

[*He starts to exercise gently, bending his knees and touching his toes.*]

I must do this for my circulation. If I was free, not like I am today, but properly free, for always—they know! It would be something they couldn't hold off, not like your Mosleys and your Jordans, your Buster Mitfords ... I don't know who these people are. They're nothing. Imitators, jokes. Hitler was an original. [*with German pronunciation*] O-rig-inal.

I heard him first in Munich. I joined immediately. I was part of the *Bierkeller Putsch*. That's when I got my first experience of prison, in Landsberg, with Hitler. We were together. We worked, we wrote; there were many things we hammered out; I took them down. You see, when I was at University, I studied under the great Professor Haushofer. Look, you must understand, because I know, you see. I get the newspapers. I read the *Daily Telegraph*. It's a good newspaper—bit too broad-minded, but it's a good newspaper. And I know that you're all absorbed in the Third Reich: your films, your television programmes, one after another; and then your magazines and your books, Toland and Shirer, and even Albert Speer now—I'm not supposedly allowed to read them, but you do—because you all so love, secretly, *secretly*, deep in your hearts, you love the Third Reich!

We had ideas. We had solutions. We had a dream—we dared to dream! We dared to make that dream a reality! That was a crime. Many people died for that crime ... that dream ... that crime.

Haushofer taught me—he didn't commit suicide till later—that a country must be big enough to accommodate its people, its culture.

Listen to this.

[*He pulls out a piece of paper.*]

[*indicating spectacles, which he puts on*] Plastic: so I can't cut myself.

[*He reads:*] "The foreign policy of a People's State must first of all bear in mind the duty of securing the existence of the race which is incorporated in this State. And this must be done by establishing a healthy and natural proportion between the number and growth of the population on the one hand and the extent and resources of the territory they inhabit on the other. The balance must be such that it accords with the vital necessities of the people."

Sometimes it is said that I wrote that. It's not possible.

It comes from the Führer's own book. [*with a canny look*] I just made a note of it from memory.

"Only a sufficiently large space on this earth can assure the independent existence of a people."

We believed that. Nobody believes it now. It has nothing to do with your colour problem, your Irish problem? The Middle East problem? No, no, of course not. Such thoughts are only a part of German criminality. Nobody else has ever tried to create a proportion between their population and their area of national territory.

We had to throw off the yoke of Versailles ...

[*He breaks off with stomach pains.*]

... to gain the power, the, the political power equal to our past as members of the highest species of humanity on this earth.

[*More stomach pains.*]

It was necessary that we push to the East. Where the people are subhuman: the Russian people.—You want proof that they're subhuman? Just look at them! They are not formed like proper people, like children of God. A flat-faced race of serfs, fit only for slavery; no wonder they took to Communism.

[*In sudden anger he slaps his hand violently on the desk.*]

They are the reason I am still kept in prison.

[*Pause.*]

[*more calmly*] Oh, some of the guards are all right, I suppose. Stepan tries to be helpful: stupid peasant, but he doesn't mean any harm. But they are the enemy! I don't talk to them. I don't afford them the privilege of being noticed. They are beneath notice. They are the enemy.

They're your enemy too, you know that. You don't like it said too often—nowadays—but you know it.

We should have been left free to smash them during the War. Then their lands and their hordes could have been

put to good use in the service of civilized, truly civilized
Volk. If Churchill hadn't refused to see me when I made
my historic journey, there would have been no need for
his famous telegram after the War. Oh, he knew where
the threat was, Churchill, but he didn't have the courage
at the time to face up to it. And so you had the Cold War,
and Cuba, and Korea, and Vietnam and all your other
troubles. Now I think you're being kicked out of Africa.
You're even losing ground in space ... [*He chuckles.*] ... to
the meddlesome Communists. Their space shuttle I find
fascinating. It's a great achievement coping with weight-
lessness for so long; and producing new alloys not possible
in our atmosphere: the technicalities of that interest
me.

But all of that could have been swept away, annihilated,
crushed under the heel of our vision, if you people hadn't
persisted. Instead, the greatest leader of men this century
has seen, perhaps the greatest in all time, was thwarted.
It was my honour to serve him, but he was the Leader.
He was a genius. He gave the German people a pride in
their nation, in place of that Allied spitoon, the Treaty of
Versailles; he gave starving men work; in place of social
and political chaos he established order, absolute order.
Troublesome minorities were dealt with. They were
sent to ...

> [*He breaks off, realizing he has said more than he
> intended.*]

No! No! They were ... I forget. I'm an old man, I don't
remember!

> [*He is psychosomatically rescued by a bad attack of
> stomach cramps.*]

We ... We ... Oh, my guts ...! We passed laws. Yes,
that's it, we passed laws. Oh, the pain! I don't remember!

> [*He howls, bends double, and falls backwards to
> the floor.*]

Milch, milch! Where's my bag?

> [*The attack is prolonged and he whimpers on the floor,
> finally dragging his plastic bag from the desk. He
> drinks from the milk container during the following:*]

It's milk. I have to line my stomach. It's not true. What
I said just now. That they try to poison me. Maybe one
time they did, but not any more. I have an ulcer. You
call it a ... perforated ulcer—yes? When the strain is too
much, it punishes me; or when I get excited. Where's
the chair?

> [*Painfully, and with difficulty, he hoists himself into
> the nearest chair.*]

I don't like showing too much emotion. It is not becoming
in a man. But sometimes I find it hard to repress when I
call to mind the Führer's vision—

A great nation, a great people, a great race, united in
devotion and obedience and glory, clean in mind and
healthy in body, purified through music, architecture,
sport; through the shared struggle to overthrow all who
oppose us!

German culture would have become world culture,
freed from decadent influences, shared by Aryan people
everywhere. There would have been no room for what
there is today: craven democracies slavering before
pornographers, and money-grubbers, and strikers *und so
weiter*, yielding ground the whole of the time to the ruthless
hands and dead minds of Communism. All these men
with feminine hair—how can you want that? Is football
hooliganism, and street mugging, and student rebellion,
is that freedom, the freedom you want? The Führer used
those sort of energies in the service of his vision. Because
he knew that the only true, complete freedom is in
obedience to a cause. The Catholic Church knows that,
too—I give them that.

Hitler gave us the cause. As a philosopher, general,

artist, statesman, orator, he was supreme! I don't know why he didn't succeed.

I think it was because the people under him weren't good enough. They didn't obey his orders; they worked behind his back. Nobody should do things behind the Leader's back. Especially such a great Leader as ... And because of the War in the West. If I had managed to end that, things would have been very different.

Germany would have had a golden future.

You might have done better, too. But you were too proud: you call the Germans arrogant—which country in the whole world is so arrogant it calls itself Great, huh? Only one. Great Britain. That's not arrogance? I put the whole of my career in the balance—and it was a Great career—and secretly, without the Führer knowing anything about it, I come to arrange peace, and what happens? Churchill is too weak to see me. Too afraid of his American allies. We would have guaranteed your Empire. Your American friends worked very hard to see it destroyed. Lend-lease. [*He laughs.*] Lend-lease! Maybe you don't feel so great now. And that was your great leader's work.

Churchill. What did he know? He made pictures but he knew nothing of painting, nothing. You ask Mr Sutherland. I know, I read about it. You ask Mr G. Sutherland. And when Churchill wrote books, somebody else had to write them. Is that a great leader? Hitler wrote all of *Mein Kampf*! Including the chapters I wrote.

So, who are the great leaders? Roosevelt, who tricked you out of your power? Nixon, Johnson? Ask the people of Vietnam, the people of Kampuchea. Jimmy Carter? Ask anybody!

Well then, how about Napoleon? Or Caesar? And what fraction of the earth's population did they have to destroy in order to achieve lasting fame and the dawn of a new civilization? Look at the Popes. Look at your Kings through history. Are they vilified because they require men to die for what they believed in?

Was Stalin kept in power in Russia because he was so good? Was it his kindness and honesty and gentle ways that made him a fit man to judge *me*? Or Hirohito in Japan—he took all those oaths of loyalty and he's still there!

You allowed Stalin to overrun half Europe and crush countries with more art, civilization, more ... more good blood than his animal hordes could ever understand or imitate.

You let America kick your colonies from under you, and now you hand your markets on a plate to the Japanese, while you listen to the soft blandishments of your politicians who comb their hair in public, and you condemn *me*, who risked everything and lost, to hold out the palm of peace to you! Is that justice?

You, too, have the blood of deaths of millions on your hands.

But I read in the newspapers now that the British people did not know. What about the soldiers who rounded them up with bayonets, the sailors who transported them, the civil servants who arranged it all, the diplomats who urged the Americans to do the same with *their* Cossacks, the English Lord who masterminded it? It is your lesson that obeying orders is no defence. It is your law—not mine—that there is corporate responsibility for national crimes.

Where is the Englishman who gave his life to oppose this known policy of mass extermination? Where are your Stauffenbergs, your Kreisau Circle? Where is the citizen of Great Britain, who, for his part in this offence against humanity, is now approaching his fortieth year in prison? Or his thirtieth? Or even his first! And that is justice!

> [*In a fury* HESS *stamps to the back of the stage and slaps the wall. After some time he turns to face the audience once more.*]

Pardon. I ask pardon. I must not shout at people, it's not allowed. It was not my intention to upset you, or to behave in an insulting fashion. I am an old man. And too much has been asked of me. How can I give up the dream I once had, when I am allowed nothing else to put in its place? When I return there tonight—tomorrow—there will be no other occasion that I shall go out through Spandau Gate. The coffin and the quicklime await me there. For what should I repent? I shall never be set free. Do you seriously think that a man can survive decade upon decade alone in a cell when he has renounced everything that he believed in and worked for? To be sane in such conditions—and I have never been mad!— you need faith, inner convictions, inner strength. Prison for a long time can never do anything except confirm a man in the ways that brought him there. For it to be otherwise he must propose for himself a future in which he passes each succeeding day in rejection of the person he was before imprisonment. That leaves him in a limbo— as prison is—not permitted to make any contribution to human thought or action, without even the foundation ... the ... the sheet-anchor, of a past. And if the sentence is so long that he can see no end to it, that leaves him with no past, no present, no future. It's not possible! Martyr- dom to a cause is not a choice. Long imprisonment makes it an inevitability.

I wonder, though, at the forces which move us toward our individual destinies.

I remember when I was wandering round München,

er, Munich, ney? in the bleak May weather of 1941, with
my faithful Pintsch at my side, I wasn't thinking that I
would never see the city again. Beautiful city! I had
made my decision, and when I make such a decision it is
unalterable, but it was no impulse, no sudden flash. It
was logical and it was right.

One of your cheap propaganda broadcasters—I
apologize, he was not English. American, I think. Well,
it doesn't matter! He spoke on the BBC. I heard him
when I was waiting in England. He said I came to *see*
humanity. He was wrong. I believe I came to *save*
humanity!

After all, in the long run, it would have saved lives.
Russia would have been quickly defeated if all our might
had been thrown against her. And we wanted no harsh
treaty with you. Hitler didn't want to do a Versailles to
you. I know. We talked about it in Landsberg, and again
not long before I went.

But it was important that nobody knew about my plan,
not the Führer, not Ilse even, not my adjutant Pintsch,
nobody. Then if I succeeded, I had served my country.
If I failed, I could be disowned. And Germany would not
be weakened. I still think of that as courage, not as
stupidity.

So I wrote two letters explaining what I was doing, and
when the weather got better I hid one of them among
Wolf-Rüdiger's toys, so that my wife would find it later,
and I gave one of them to my adjutant, Pintsch, to take to
Hitler at Berchtesgaden.

Then I went to Augsburg, to the Messerschmitt airfield.
My old friend Willi Messerschmitt! He often lent me a
plane for a journey, or just so I could put in my hours of
flying and not get rusty. This time he gave me an Me 110.
It was new, of course, but I soon mastered the different
control layout. Well no, it was a new version, I should

say. As an escort fighter in the Zerstörer Class it had been around for a year or two. But now it had been completely stripped. Everything unnecessary had been taken out so it could operate as a reconnaissance plane, with a range of about one thousand kilometres—one kilometre for every year of the Reich, ha! The cockpit was so as the Junkers fighter, you know? The canopy was a long bubble on top of the fuselage, like a caterpillar facing backwards, with the gun pointing out for the caterpillar's antenna. There was no gunner for me, though. I was alone.

I taxied to the runway and felt the powerful thrust of the twin engines as I sped along and up into the open sky. The hangars disappeared behind me, and I banked onto a route north-north-west which would take me straight to the Dutch coast. Here, I show you.

[*He places the chair downstage left.*]

Here is Augsburg. München is there. [*indicating a point further downstage left of the chair*] This is England. [*pointing to desk*] And I am going here. [*placing plastic milk container up right on the desk*] This is the English Channel ... [*walking to downstage left of the chair again, with an expansive gesture*] ... and all this is Germany. Or is under our control.

[*He moves the chair fractionally.*]

So. I go in a straight line. Dee-rect!

[*He starts to walk slowly, arms out like a child playing aeroplanes, along the line of his route.*]

Below, the houses and trees and animals diminish into playthings. I feel very calm. I pass over towns and villages, some strange, some known to me. Visibility? Good. No difficult winds. The colours of the fields, the sky, have a clarity, a ... translucence which is serenely beautiful. Everyone should learn to fly. It's the greatest experience for a man.

[*He breaks off, overcome by the memory. Then resumes:*]

Now, I am coming to the sea. The sun is going down. The sky, a blue-glowing crystal tinged with fire.

Ahead of me is the English coast, and for the first time the weather forecasters are right! Thick, hazy cloud, very low down. You see, they said there would be cloud all the way, but behind me is all—ach! There is a Spitfire on my tail. Not a whole squadron, just one. Quickly, quickly, open the throttle, put down the nose and dive for that cloudbank, thank God for it! Now my engines are screaming as my speed is going up and up.

> [*Now he demonstrates, using his left hand alone as the aircraft.*]

500 kilometres an hour, 600—that's the maximum flying speed but I'm in a dive—700, 750, and I'm there. Quickly level out. Keep all the speed I can. Now I don't just head in a straight line. Where the cloud goes, I go too. This way, that way, edging towards Scotland, keeping very, very low, hopping over the hedges and grazing the rooftops.

The Spitfire has lost me. So. But there may be others. I mustn't take any risks. So I screw my eyes and keep just a few metres above the ground.

> [*He perches on the downstage end of the desk, which now becomes his aircraft.*]

This makes me tired, but there is no more trouble. Now at last I can see the west coast of Schottland. I fly out to it and then turn back so as to make a dead reckoning. I check my maps and find where I want for the estate of the Duke of Hamilton.

How to land? That's not easy. It's dark now and I don't know the terrain. Maybe I crash, which would not be good.

Take her up to 2,000 feet, that's the answer. Put her at cruising speed. Check my buckles. Force open the canopy ... and ... jump!

[*He lowers himself to the floor and does a couple of knee-bends.*]

It hurt when I landed: injured my leg. There was a farmhouse very near, luckily, and the people were kind. They offered me a cup of tea. I said, no, just a glass of water. I tell them I want to speak with the Duke of Hamilton. He will take me to the King of England and then we can make peace. But the people don't understand. Maybe they don't know who I am—I don't dress like Göring. Göring was a great man. But sometimes he look like a great woman. I was just in the uniform of a Captain, so perhaps the people didn't realize. You know something, I still have that uniform jacket. I smuggle it out of Spandau when they bring me to the hospital—I will get it!

[*He sets off and then, surprisingly, stops.*]

No! No! You go away: have cup of tea, glass of beer, what you want. Come back in fifteen minutes, and I will show you.—If the police or the Army Security haven't found out where we are, that is. When they get here it will be like when I was in Schottland before—what I was telling you just now—they won't let me talk; they won't let the truth be known. Their friends, their foreign ... Bolshevik friends wouldn't permit it.

But now we are having a good laugh at them—yes? I get my historic uniform.

[*He goes off in a lively way.*]

END OF ACT ONE

ACT TWO

HESS *re-enters with a bundle very apparently shoved inside his dressing gown. He peers round the audience.*

No one has come? No police? No military? So, I show you.
> [*He brings out a World War II Luftwaffe Captain's tunic and holds it up.*]

Nice, yes? Very ... [*He smells it.*] Hm, mothballs. Moment now.
> [*He removes his dressing gown and attempts to pull on the tunic. He is unable to get the second arm in and seeks help from someone in his audience. The dressing complete, he stands to attention.*]

Hauptmann Hess! This is how your country first saw me. Now you see me in it again. Funny isn't it? It isn't even my jacket. I just borrowed it off a peg in Augsburg. Maybe they bury me in it now. After all, my life was ended from the first second I put it on. Who would have guessed it? Who would have guessed that the shirt of Nessus would smell of mothballs.

The English were good to me when I arrived; but not good enough! When I came out of Military Hospital with my leg that I hurt in the parachute jump, I saw your Duke of Hamilton, and your important diplomat, Mr Kirkpatrick; and once or twice I saw Dr Guthrie, who was really the famous political leader, Lord Simon. He didn't look well. He had glassy eyes. Maybe it was the English food. All that Wolsey Pie. I don't know why he called himself

33

Dr Guthrie—he needed a doctor, not me. Still, I was treated quite properly; not as a Reichsminister, but at least as an officer, as a Captain—because of this. They didn't let me see Churchill, though. That was my fault. I said we would not deal with the existing warmongering government. Churchill would have to go! That was an error. Why should he go because I say so? Well, he didn't. I did.

They took me off to prisoner-of-war camp. To several camps, one after another, a grand tour of Nissen huts; I was in different places in Wales, then Aldershot, and first London. Aldershot was sandy, not so cold and wet as Wales. Meanwhile my adjutant Pintsch had gone to the Berghof to give my letter to the Führer. Speer was waiting to see Hitler, but he let Pintsch go in first. He told me about it later—at Nürnberg, I think. Hitler was not pleased. He shouted for Bormann who called for Göring, who said that I would never make it—with the journey, I mean, that I would crash in the North Sea. Then, when the British Government announced that I had arrived, Hitler told everyone that I was mad, crazy. Does a crazy man successfully fly an aircraft further than the head of the Luftwaffe thinks possible, and then in alien territory he has never seen before bale out within ten miles of his exact target—in the dark! Is that how a crazy man does things? When I make up my mind to do something I carry it through to the end. And I was right. If I'd gone back in 1945 Hitler wouldn't have shot me. He would have shaken me by the hand and said, Comrade, you were right. He would have had to use his good hand for shaking, of course.

But all my efforts came to nothing. Or rather they came to this. This is my destiny. You can't fight that; it's decided for you. All you can do is fulfil your task like a man.

Before I flew from Augsburg, before even my friend Albrecht Haushofer—he was the son of the great Professor Haushofer—well, before he sent off the peace-feeler letters to England—you see, he knew Duke Hamilton, I never met him, so all the initial laying-of-the-ground work I did through my friend Albrecht; before even this, a great fortune-teller told me that I would walk through ancient castles in England in the search for an end to the War. He didn't say one of them would be the Tower of London! So you see I would have had to come anyway. And even if I had planned the very opposite, if I had been against any trip to England, instead of accepting my duty to mankind, I would still have had to come.

I tell you why. [*intimately, sitting on the chair far downstage left*] Every day for the two months before I arrived, on a little airstrip outside—oh, what's it called ... it's a place for holidays of the English south coast ... er ... Volkstown. No, wait a bit, Lympne! Yes, that's it: Lympne Aerodrome, near Volkstown. Well, there, every night for the two months before I arrived, airmen under the command of Leigh Mallory, the RAF Chief, practised shooting the tail off a Focke-Wulf Condor, which had supposedly just landed. They were on constant alert for when the real Focke-Wulf Condor landed. There was a van waiting there, a Smith's Crisps van, ready to drive the occupant of this plane, which now couldn't fly away any more with its tail blown off, direct to Downing Street. Who was this occupant to be?

[*He looks round the audience and preens.*]

Rudolf Hess!

You see, there was a pilot who sometimes flew me—and other high-ups—who was also working for you. I find it hard to believe, but there. He should have been shot. Well, he was shot, but not until later. He was going to kidnap me and bring me to England.

[He rises and looks for a reaction. Surprised that there is none, he goes on.]

You don't know about that? It's true. The officer in charge of the operation, under Mallory, was called, I think, Squadron-Leader Montgomery; the officer in charge of the guns was Lieutenant Hobley, R.A. I learned the details when I was a prisoner-of-war—who says I suffer from amnesia! The practices at Lympne were called off the day after I landed by parachute. They were no longer necessary. But either way, you see, I should have become your guest. It was determined!

But then you don't treat me right. Oh, while the War was on everything was in order and nice. I meet people and talk to them. I eat cucumber sandwiches, and your officers explain me about cricket. But when the War is over I should have been sent back to Germany. Well, I was sent back to Germany. But I should have taken over the running of the Reich; with the Control Commissioners of the Allies to assist me of course, we could not have done things without them. Hitler was dead! I was the Deputy Führer. No other government had been elected. It was therefore my duty to lead the German people in their darkest hour. Instead I was prevented. How could the German people believe in the good faith of National Socialism when the party is stopped from governing? That is not right.

When I was returned to Germany they took me straight to Nürnberg. It was strange to see so many old faces again: Göring, von Ribbentrop, Funk *und so weiter*. They all looked older. Except for Göring—he looked younger, and not so fat. And he smelt of carbolic instead of cologne. We were all in cells, quite little ones, with lights on all the time and a flimsy table and chair which would fall down if you jumped on them, they were so weak. Everything was taken away. Braces, shoe-laces, razor blades. That's not in the Geneva Convention! I was a prisoner-of-war of the British and a high-ranking political leader. I was treated like a common thief.

The Nürnberg Trial was illegal.

How can I be tried by the Americans and the Russians? I was out of the War before they were ever in it: at no moment of my participation were America and Russia on the opposite side to me—so how can I have offended them? My dealings should have been solely with the British. And to them I came on a peace mission. I broke no laws in England. And the only law I broke in Germany was coming on the very same peace mission. For the British that is a crime?

The Nürnberg Trial should not have taken place. Or if it did take place, I should not have been a part of it. We should not have been called to account by other countries for ... internal matters. Revenge should not put on a pretty dress and call itself Justice!

That was my view at the time. That was the decision I came to on the matter, and when I come to such a decision, it is irrevocable!

It was therefore necessary to ignore what was happening, to refuse to give it countenance. That is why I would not allow my family to see me in my degradation. That is why, alone of my comrades, I did not turn to religion. It would have been weakness. It would have been dishonest. I made my career without God; when so many people were so busy unmaking my career, it would have been cheating to turn to God then. And that is why I decided to lose my memory. To blot it all out. It wasn't easy, I can tell you.

The trial went on for nine months. Every day, from nine in the morning till noon, from two in the afternoon until five. And at other times they sent psychiatrists to test me; they used hypnosis, and I just pretended to go under; guards watched me every minute and every hour, and all the tricks in the book were used to try and catch me out. But I fooled them all!

The worst moment was when they brought my secretary to see me—not Bormann, he was a different kind of secretary—no, the lady who did my typing, Hildegard. We met face to face and I just looked straight through her. She burst into tears. It was very hard for me then not to show any expression, and I'm sorry that I upset her. But it had to be. And it was that that finally convinced them. Ha, they said, Hess has lost his mind. Well, why not? Hitler told the whole world I was crazy. Now it suited me to be crazy. But like Shakespeare says, I was only crazy north-north-west. [*He chuckles to himself.*] North-north-west was the route I had flown.

So every day, when we sat in the big court room, with the eight judges, and all the clerks and prosecutors, translators and counsel, the cameramen, the guards in their battle hats, and the might of the Third Reich huddled together like refugees in hand-me-down suits, I pretended it was not happening. Or rather, I pretended to pretend it was not happening.

I read books. All sorts of books. Novels, travel books, biographies. One, by Kurt Faber, had a strangely appropriate title, I remember: *A Globetrotter's Last Adventures*. I don't remember the others now. I very seldom listened to the earphones with the translation of the proceedings. Ha! Everybody said: Hess is mad, he pays no attention to the trial. But I had duped them again! The evidence and the questioning were in one of four languages: French, English, German, Russian. French I learn in school and I speak in Switzerland. My English is good—yes? Yes! German is my native tongue. With my nose buried in a book, I knew what was happening: it's not your eyes you use for listening. And I didn't need a translation of what the Russians had to say. They wanted to hang me from the start, I knew that. So why should I listen to them? Oh, I knew what was happening all right. I didn't lose my memory as a ruse to save my life. I knew we should all be killed. Oddly enough I didn't listen to the verdict, I was so sure. It wasn't till I went below to the cells that someone tapped me on the shoulder and told me I had been given life. Life! No, I lost my memory so that I could not answer the charges.

[HESS *begins to lose mental and emotional equilibrium.*]

I cannot ... address myself ... to the charges. I am not a schoolboy to be thrashed in public. I am the Deputy Führer of the German people! No. I'm an old man.

[*Pause.*]

[*calmly*] We sat in two rows. Göring on the right, then me, von Ribbentrop, Keitel, Rosenberg, Frank, who wouldn't take off his sunglasses, Frick, Streicher, Funk ... [*He gropes for the final name.*] ... Schacht, in that jacket with the funny collar. Behind us, a little higher, like in a lecture theatre—like here—sat Dönitz and the smaller fry.

The court room ... [*He looks round tensely during this, unsure whether he may not actually be back there.*] ... it was the main one of the Bavarian Central Courts of Justice, the very room where a year before the plotters against Hitler's life had been tried, had been changed. It had been made so that it could hold pressmen and visitors.

[*Despite the visitors who make up his audience, HESS decides he has not been returned to the courtroom, and shakes his head twice in rejection of the idea.*]

The Judges were dressed up like for a comic opera. The Russians in uniforms with wide flat shoulders; the Americans and the British in big gowns; the French in frills, and lace. Only the music was missing. If the trial was really about justice, and not a continuation of the

War, why was there no German Judge? No neutral Judge, a Swiss or a ... eh? No! The victors prosecuted, and the victors judged!

It took two November days for the indictments to be read. Two whole days to recite the details of the charges. There were four:

> Conspiracy for war
> Crimes against peace
> War crimes
> Crimes against humanity

I don't know of any country in the world where you find such criminal charges on the statute books. They were invented for the purpose. If it's a crime to make war, where is the country whose history shows it to be guiltless? What's a crime against peace, except making war? All war, not just ours.. Oh, we marched into Czechoslovakia, yes. So has Russia since. And into Hungary, and a lot of other places.

War crimes? I don't know. I wasn't a General. Was the Vice-President of the United States responsible for Lieutenant Calley? Is it the British Prime Minister's fault that Colonel Callan behaved in Africa like an animal? It was not I who appointed Kaltenbrunner to head the Gestapo, it was Himmler who appointed me to be Hitler's adjutant in '29, so you see ...

> [*He hurries on, suddenly realizing this piece of news hardly helps his argument.*]

All war is full of dreadful things. That is the nature of war. Ask the British Tommy with his flame-thrower. Ask the people of Hiroshima and Dresden and Hamburg. Not just the people of Coventry and Lidice ... Well, you can't ask the people of Lidice ... I didn't order these things. War is a filthy activity, and everyone who touches it is besmirched. Not just me, not just the Germans.

> [*Pause. Then quietly*:]

There was only one real crime: crime against humanity. I was acquitted of that charge.

Anti-Semitism was not the provenance solely of Nazi Germany. It was the apotheosis of European history and of widely held Western attitudes and ideology. We didn't invent it.

What about Fagin, Shylock? The villains in John Buchan are the Jews. When they are not the Germans. The villains for Goethe, our greatest writer, were also the Jews. The Russians persecute them, the Arabs try to drive them out. Plenty of Polishmen, Frenchmen, Dutchmen *volunteered* to round them up.

During my time in power I always used my influence to protect the wife of the great Professor Haushofer. She was a Jew. My good friend Albrecht was half a Jew. And I worked very hard to bring down Julius Streicher, who was the most virulent anti-Semite, a revolting mind in a revolting body. Many times I asked Hitler to have him dismissed. Hitler turned me down. Then, finally, with Liebel's help, I had him brought before the Party's highest court. He was found guilty of gross corruption and disgraced. Hitler tried to sack the Judge—but he was Bormann's father-in-law, so he survived. And Streicher lived on as a pariah, until he came to Nürnberg and suddenly discovered that he thought the Jews were very nice people. Then the Allies stretched his neck. Which was always very short.

In the courtroom, we were shown a film—it was the only time they put out the lights.

> [*At a small hand gesture from* HESS *the lights are snapped out, leaving only the barest glimmer by which his shape and face can be made out.*]

Dachau, Malthausen, Ravensbrück, Belsen, Auschwitz. My brother was taken to one of those. Dry skin draped and flapping like worn cotton curtains over the whitened bones of once ... supple bodies. Withered eyes. Legs that would snap in a breeze. I watched every frame. No more jokes like earlier with Göring. I was transfixed. I had never seen such ... obscenity.

> [*He bows his head. The lights creep up again, fewer than before, the floor tinged with red, the rest much colder.*]

I was acquitted of crimes against humanity.

> [*Another pause.*]

I want to tell you but I can't.

> [*Pause. Then with his eyes shut:*]

I was in love with that pure fire, that lambent flame which burns eternally in the heart of the Teutonic ... I didn't mean *that.* I didn't know what it was like.

> [*Pause. Outburst:*]

Yes! I was proud to give my name to the anti-Jewish legislation of 1935. The Hess Act. I wanted it! But I'm not responsible for what happened. The Court said so. The greatest judges in the world put their heads together and said Hess has committed no crimes against humanity, isn't that enough?

My head aches. I can't sort it out in my head.

> [*He buries his head in his hands.*]

It's too late. I gave myself to Hitler's dream. It's too late. I can't bring anyone back from the dead. It's too late. How can I change, how can I repay? It's too late.

I could have done something after the War. I wanted to. My plans were quite realistic: to unite the German people in dignity and in obedience to the Allies. To close up old wounds and open no new ones. I had policies for food and transportation, for policing the State, for a free press, and for the kind of music we should have on the radio. My government was to be formed from existing ministers and from others who were at that time in concentration camps.

We were going to have a new Constitution. I hadn't decided what it was to be, but if people liked me ruling them, it would have ensured that this situation was continued.

[*He puts a chair on the table, climbs up and uses the chair as a lectern.*]

There would have been a new nationalism. Families could have been proud of their fathers, parents of their children, who died in the cause of our Homeland. Instead of wearying shame, some pride. It is hard when you have lost everything and you are not allowed to feel honour in the sacrifice.

The Reichstag would have been formed again. And I prepared a great speech to deliver at its opening, praising our lost leaders, warning against Bolshevism, and saying the things I was not permitted to say at Nürnberg!

It was found, the speech which I had written out, and all my future plans for the nation, the guards found them under the mattress in my cell. My ideas were not adopted.

Now?—I don't care!

So I feed the birds, read the newspapers, and I write to Ilse.

[*He reverses the chair and sits on it, still atop the table.*]

If the roles had been reversed, would we have behaved any differently towards you? Of course. We would have shot your leaders out of hand, Churchill, Eden, Muggeridge, Graham Greene, all of them. No trials, no pretences. We were a totalitarian state.

But you are a Christian democracy and you should behave according to *your* rules. After all, those were the rules you judged *us* by.

And maybe our action would have been kinder than yours. More honest, anyway. We never took anyone's life so *slowly* as you have taken mine.

It's all so long ago. The consequences live on, of

course, and I must not look to escape them. But I am trapped in time, unable for so many years to progress beyond the moment of my condemnation and what led to it. Is that what the world wants for me? Is it right to wish that for anybody? If there is no forgiveness without repentance, it is true too that there can be no repentance where forgiveness, by definition, is perpetually denied.

So, I am anchored in dead history, a sort of coelacanth. You know, if I were to be set free tomorrow, the most terrified person in the whole world at this event would be—me. All the same, I should like to see our little home, to rest a hand upon the shoulders of my loved ones, to feed the birds under a tree that was not planted by Grand Admiral Dönitz.

> [*He looks around blankly, no more to say. Then conversationally* :]

They must have missed me at the hospital by now. Soon they will come, the police, the soldiers, to take me back. Tomorrow I will fly to Berlin, back to the Chapel. Did you know? Since the others left I've moved into what used to be the prison Chapel. It's bigger than the other cells and there's a radiator. I had the Cross taken away. And the clock.

> [*He looks round once more, taking final stock, then gazes at the audience. An idea forms. He pulls off his jacket and throws it on the floor.*]

Perhaps I'll beat you yet.

> [*He stands and grabs the nearest rope.*]

My one chance to die a free man. That would be a good joke.

> [*He ties a thumb-knot noose and tries unsuccessfully to bring it over his head. He inserts his right arm into the noose to hold it open while he tries again. He over-balances from the table and is left suspended in the Nazi salute.*]

Oh no. Go on, laugh! Where there is no forgiveness, laugh!

> [*With difficulty he releases his wrist with his free hand.*
> *Rubbing his wrist he makes slowly for the exit.*]

Someone, telephone the authorities. Tell them, Hess has landed again. Eaglesham, that's where it was. *Eagle-sham*! Tell them, Hess wants to give up.

> [*He goes out.*]

THE END